NEVER
FORGET
...Hope

BILLY GRAHAM
ANNE GRAHAM LOTZ
MAX LUCADO

HENRI NOUWEN
CHARLES STANLEY

WITH SCRIPTURE SELECTIONS

Thomas Nelson
Since 1798

NASHVILLE   DALLAS   MEXICO CITY   RIO DE JANEIRO

Never Forget . . . Hope

© 2011 by Thomas Nelson, Inc.

Published in Nashville, Tennessee, by Thomas Nelson®. Thomas Nelson is a trademark of Thomas Nelson, Inc.

Thomas Nelson, Inc., titles may be purchased in bulk for educational, business, fund-raising, or sales promotional use. For information, please e-mail NelsonMinistryServices@ ThomasNelson.com.

Unless otherwise noted, all Scripture quotations are from *The Holy Bible, New Century Version* (NCV), copyright 1987, 1988, 1991 by W Publishing Group, Nashville, TN 37214.

Scripture quotations marked (NLT) are taken from the Holy Bible, New Living Translation, copyright © 1996, 2004, 2007 by Tyndale House Foundation. Used by permission of Tyndale House Publishers, Inc., Carol Stream, Illinois 60188. All rights reserved. Scripture quotations marked (NIV) are taken from the Holy Bible, New International Versio®. NIV® Copyright © 1973, 1978, 1984 by International Bible Society. Used by permission of Zondervan Publishing House. Scripture quotations marked (NKJV) are taken from THE NEW KING JAMES VERSION. © 1982, 1992 by Thomas Nelson, Inc. Used by permission. All rights reserved. Scripture quotations marked (NRSV) are taken from The New Revised Standard Version of the Bible © 1989 by the Division of Christian Education of the National Council of Churches of Christ in the USA.

Compiled and edited by Elizabeth Kea and Beth Ryan.

ISBN-13: 9781404183322

Printed in the United States of America

11 12 13 14 15 DP 5 4 3 2 1

www.thomasnelson.com

CONTENTS

Hope

Where Is God?

God Is for You

God Is Passionate for You

Does God Care?

The Ultimate Fear

Confident Hope

Looking Forward

Never Forget

... Hope!

Excerpts from the following

A Note from the Publisher

September 11, 2001, is a day America and the world will never forget. So many lives were lost: fathers, mothers, sons, daughters, friends, companions, coworkers, and citizens of various nations. Families from around the world bear the scars of what happened that day. And while the devastations from the attacks of September 11 is unforgettable, many of us find ourselves thrust into the midst of devastating personal catastrophes, and we wonder how we'll cope.

The good news—even the GREAT news—is that there is HOPE to be discovered amid the rubble of tragedy. In this little book, you will find that hope. Through God's Word and selected writings from leading Christian authors, you will find answers to the hard questions of suffering, and you will discover that, in the end,

Hope

prevails and brings new life!

PREFACE

Address to the Nation
President George W. Bush
September 11, 2001

Today, our fellow citizens, our way of life, our very freedom, came under attack in a series of deliberate and deadly terrorist acts. The victims were in airplanes, or in their offices; secretaries, businessmen and women, military and federal workers; moms and dads, friends and neighbors. Thousands of lives were suddenly ended by evil, despicable acts of terror.

The pictures of airplanes flying into buildings, fires burning, huge structures collapsing, have filled us with disbelief, terrible sadness, and a quiet, unyielding anger. These acts of mass murder were intended to frighten our nation into chaos and retreat. But they have failed; our country is strong.

A great people have been moved to defend a great nation. Terrorist attacks can shake the foundations of our biggest buildings, but they cannot touch the foundation of America. These acts shattered steel, but they cannot dent the steel of American resolve.

America was targeted for attack because we're the brightest beacon for freedom and opportunity in the world. And no one will keep that light from shining.

Today, our nation saw evil, the very worst of human nature. And we responded with the best of America—with the daring of our rescue workers, with the caring from strangers and neighbors who came to give blood and help in any way they could . . .

America and our friends and allies join with all those who want peace and security in the world, and we stand together to win the war against terrorism. Tonight, I ask for your prayers for all those who grieve, for the children whose worlds have been shattered, for all whose sense of safety and security has been threatened. And I pray they will be comforted by a power greater than any of us, spoken through the ages in Psalm 23: "Even though I walk through the valley of the shadow of death, I fear no evil, for You are with me."

This is a day when all Americans from every walk of life unite in our resolve for justice and peace. America has stood down enemies before, and we will do so this time. None of us will ever forget this day. Yet, we go forward to defend freedom and all that is good and just in our world.

HOPE

Billy Graham
(excerpt from
Hope for the Troubled Heart)

"This is the generation that will pass through the fire. It is the generation . . . 'under the gun.' This is the tormented generation. This is the generation destined to live in the midst of crisis, danger, fear, and death. We are a people under sentence of death, waiting for the date to be set. We sense that something is about to happen. We know that things cannot go on as they are. History has reached an impasse. We are now on a collision course. Something is about to give."

I wrote this in 1965!

At that time few of us thought that the world could get much worse and survive. I was wrong. In many ways the world has gotten worse, and we have survived. But we are a world in pain—a world that suffers collectively from the violence of nature and man, and a world that suffers individually from personal heartache.

Because we have instant communication today, our planet has shrunk to the size of a computer screen or smaller. Although husbands and wives, children and parents, have trouble communicating, we can watch a war as it is happening before our eyes. A comfortable room can be turned into a foreign battlefield or a street riot with the push of a button.

In my travels over the decades, I have found that people are the same the world over. However, in recent years I find that there is an increasing problem that I would sum up in the word "hopeless." It may be because we get news of troubles, problems, disasters, wars, etc., instantaneously in comparison to years ago when it might have taken weeks, months, or even years to hear of an event. But there's something else even more insidious. People in the most affluent societies are feeling this sense of despair and hopelessness.

Perhaps the greatest psychological, spiritual, and medical need that all people have is the need for hope. Dr. McNair Wilson, the famous cardiologist, remarked in his autobiography, *Doctor's Progress*, "Hope is the medicine I use more than any other—hope can cure nearly anything."

I remember years ago that Dr. Harold Wolff, professor of medicine at Cornell University Medical College and associate professor of psychiatry, said, "Hope, like faith and a purpose in life, is medicinal. This is not exactly a statement of belief, but a conclusion proved by a meticulously controlled scientific experiment."When suffering hits us personally, that is the common cry. *Why Me? What's the reason?*

For man without faith in a personal God, reactions to painful situations are as varied as pain itself. Without God's guidance, our response to suffering is a futile attempt to find solutions to conditions that cannot be solved. We are plummeting into a world where, in spite of wonder drugs and medical breakthroughs, suffering will become more intense. For all suffering, we know, is not physical. Today, more than ever, we need to know how to find strength to live life to its fullest to have hope even in the midst of tragedy and loss.

Some see God as a harsh father, waiting to punish His children when they do something wrong. Others perceive God as unable to handle the evil on earth, or indifferent to the suffering caused by it. God's love is unchangeable; He knows exactly what we are and loves us anyway. In fact, He created us because He wanted other creatures in His image upon whom He could pour out His love and who would love Him in return. He also wanted that love to be voluntary, not forced, so He gave us freedom of choice, the ability to say yes or no in our relationship to Him. God does not want mechanized love, the kind that says we must love God because it's what our parents demand or our church preaches. Only voluntary love satisfies the Heart of God.

On the human level, we frequently love the one who loves us. In the spiritual realm, people do not grasp the overwhelming love of a holy God, but we can understand God's love by getting to know Him through Jesus Christ. No one can grasp the love of the God of the universe without knowing His Son.

Many were amazed when they saw him beaten and bloodied, so disfigured one would scarcely know he was a person . . .

. . . He was oppressed and treated harshly yet he never said a word. He was led as a lamb to the slaughter. And as a sheep is silent before the shearers, he did not open his mouth. From prison and trial they led him away to his death. But who among the people realized that he was dying for their sins— that He was suffering their punishment? He had done no wrong and he never deceived anyone . . . and because of what he experienced, my righteous servant will make it possible for many to be counted righteous, for he will bear all their sins. (From the book of Isaiah 53 NLT, and written 700 years before Christ was born.)

Neither death nor life, nor angels nor principalities nor powers, nor things present nor things to come, nor height nor depth, nor any other created thing, shall be able to separate us from the love of God which is in Christ Jesus our Lord (Romans 8:38–39 NKJV).

WHERE IS GOD?

Max Lucado
(excerpt from *America Looks Up*)

Many people today are wondering how God could allow the tragedy of September 11, 2001, and other tragedies happening around the world today. What could he be thinking? Is God really in control? Can we trust him to run the universe if he would allow terrorists to take the lives of so many people? . . . Why does he allow natural disasters like earthquakes, hurricanes, and floods to take so many lives? . . .

It is important to recognize that God dwells in a different realm. He occupies another dimension. "My thoughts are not your thoughts, nor are your ways My ways," says the Lord. "For as the heavens are higher than the earth, so are My ways higher than your ways, and My thoughts than your thoughts" (Isaiah 55:8–9 NKJV).

Make special note of the word *like*. God's thoughts are not our thoughts, nor are they even *like* ours. We aren't even in the same neighborhood. We're thinking, *Preserve the body;* He's thinking, *Save the soul.* We dream of a pay raise. He dreams of raising the dead. We avoid pain and seek peace. God uses pain to bring peace. "I'm going to live before I die," we resolve. "Die so you can live," he instructs. We love what rusts. He loves what endures. We rejoice at our successes. He rejoices at our confessions. We show our children the Nike star with the million-dollar smile and say, "Be like Mike." God points to the crucified carpenter with bloody lips and a torn side and says, "Be like Christ."

Our thoughts are not like God's thoughts. Our ways are not like his ways. He has a different agenda. He dwells in a different dimension. He lives on another plane.

The heavens tell the glory of God,
And the skies announce what his hands have made.
Day after day they tell the story;
Night after night they tell it again.
They have no speech or words;
They have no voice to be heard.
But their message goes out through all the world;
Their words go everywhere on earth.

Psalm 19:1–4 NCV

Nature is God's workshop. The sky is his résumé. The universe is his calling card. You want to know who God is? See what he has done. You want to know his power? Take a look at his creation. Curious about his strength? Pay a visit to his home address: 1 Billion Starry Sky Avenue. Want to know his size? Step out into the night and stare at starlight emitted one million years ago . . .

He is untainted by the atmosphere of sin, unbridled by the time line of history, unhindered by the weariness of the body.

What controls you doesn't control him. What troubles you doesn't trouble him. What fatigues you doesn't fatigue him. Is an eagle disturbed by traffic? No, he rises about it. Is the whale perturbed by a hurricane? Of course not; he plunges beneath it. Is the lion flustered by the mouse standing directly in his way? No, he steps over it.

How much more is God able to soar above, plunge beneath, and step over the troubles of the earth? "What is impossible with man is possible with God" (see Matthew 19:26). Our questions betray our lack of understanding:

* How can God be everywhere at one time? (Who says God is bound by a body?)

* How can God hear all the prayers that come to him? (Perhaps his ears are different from yours.)

* How can God be the Father, the Son, and the Holy Spirit? (Could it be that heaven has a different set of physics than earth?)

If people down here won't forgive me, how much more am I guilty before a holy God? (Oh, just the opposite. God is always able to give grace when we humans can't—he invented it.)

How vital that we pray, armed with the knowledge that God is in heaven. Pray with any lesser conviction, and our prayers are timid, shallow, and hollow. Look up and see what God has done, and watch how your prayers are energized.

This knowledge gives us confidence as we face the uncertain future. We know that he is in control of the universe, and so we can rest secure. But important also is the knowledge that this God in heaven has chosen to bend an ear toward earth to see our sorrow and hear our prayers. He is not so far above us that he is not touched by our tears.

Though we may not be able to see his purpose or his plan, the Lord of heaven is on his throne and in firm control of the universe and our lives. So we entrust him with our future. We entrust him with our very lives.

Let all that I am wait quietly before God,
      for my hope is in him.
He alone is my rock and my salvation,
      my fortress where I will not be shaken.
My victory and honor come from God alone.
He is my refuge, a rock where no enemy can
      reach me.
O my people, trust in him at all times.
Pour out your heart to him,
      for God is our refuge.

Psalm 62:5–8 NLT

"Look at my Servant, whom I have chosen.
      He is my Beloved, who pleases me.
I will put my Spirit upon him,
      and he will proclaim justice to the nations.
He will not fight or shout
      or raise his voice in public.
He will not crush the weakest reed
      or put out a flickering candle.
Finally he will cause justice to be victorious.
And his name will be the hope
      of all the world."

Matthew 12:18–29 NLT

★ ★ ★ ★ ★

GOD IS FOR YOU

Max Lucado
(excerpt from *America Looks Up*)

These questions are not new to you. You've asked them before. In the night you've asked them; in anger you've asked them. The doctor's diagnosis brought them to the surface, as did the court's decision, the phone call from the bank, and the incomprehensible tragedies that occur in our world. The questions are probes of pain and problem and circumstance. No, the questions are not new, but maybe the answers are.

If God is for us, who can be against us? (Romans 8:31 NIV)

The question is simply "Who can be against us?" You could answer that one. Who is against you? Disease, inflation, a recession, corruption, exhaustion. Calamities confront, and fears imprison. Were the question "Who can be against us?" we could list our foes much easier than we could fight them. But that is not the question. The question is, IF GOD IS FOR US, who can be against us? . . .

God is for you. Your parents may have forgotten you, your teachers may have neglected you, your siblings may be ashamed of you, but within reach of your prayers is the Maker of the oceans. God!

God *is* for you. Not "may be," not "has been" not "was," not "would be," but "God is!" He *is* for you. Today. At this hour. At this minute. As you read this sentence. No need to wait in line or come back tomorrow. He is with you. He could not be closer than he is at this second. His loyalty won't increase if you are better nor lessen if you are worse. He *is* for you.

God is *for* you. Turn to the sidelines; that's God cheering your run. Look past the finish line; that's God applauding your steps. Listen for him in the bleachers, shouting your name. Too tired to continue? He'll carry you. Too discouraged to fight? He's picking you up. God is *for* you.

God is for *you*. Had he a calendar, your birthday would be circled. If he drove a car, your name would be on his bumper. If there's a tree in heaven, he's carved your name in the bark. We know he has a tattoo, and we know what it says. "I have written your name on my hand," he declares (Isaiah 49:16 NLT) . . .

God is with you. Knowing that, who is against you? Can death harm you now? Can disease rob your life? Can your purpose be taken or value diminished? No . . .

And when bad things happen—does God care then? Does he love me in the midst of fear? Is he with me when danger lurks?

Will God stop loving me?

That's the question. That's the concern. Oh, you don't say it; you may not even know it. But I can see it on your faces. I can hear it in your words. Did I cross the line this week? Last Tuesday when I drank vodka until I couldn't walk . . . last Thursday when my business took me where I had no business being . . . last summer when I cursed the God who made me as I stood near the grave of the child he gave me?

Did I drift too far? Wait too long? Slip too much? Was I too uncertain? Too fearful? Too angry at the pain in this world?

That's what we want to know.

Can anything separate us from the love Christ has for us?

God answered our question before we asked it. So we'd see his answer, he lit the sky with a star. So we'd hear it, he filled the night with a choir; and so we'd believe it, he did what no man had ever dreamed. He became flesh and dwelt among us.

He placed his hand on the shoulder of humanity and said, "You're something special."

If God is for us, who can ever be against us? Since he did not spare even his own Son but gave him up for us all, won't he also give us everything else? Who dares accuse us whom God has chosen for his own? No one—for God himself has given us right standing with himself. Who then will condemn us? No one—for Christ Jesus died for us and was raised to life for us, and he is sitting in the place of honor at God's right hand, pleading for us.

Can anything ever separate us from Christ's love? Does it mean he no longer loves us if we have trouble or calamity, or are persecuted, or hungry, or destitute, or in danger, or threatened with death? (As the Scriptures say, "For your sake we are killed every day; we are being slaughtered like sheep.") No, despite all these things, overwhelming victory is ours through Christ, who loved us.

(Romans 8:31–37 NLT)

GOD IS PASSIONATE FOR YOU

Max Lucado
(excerpt from *Experiencing the Heart of Jesus*)

The hand squeezing the handle was not a Roman infantryman. The force behind the hammer was not an angry mob. The verdict behind the death was not decided by jealous Jews. Jesus himself chose the nails. So the hands of Jesus opened up. Had the soldier hesitated, Jesus himself would have swung the mallet. He knew how; he was no stranger to the driving of nails. As a carpenter he knew what it took. And as a Savior he knew what it meant. He knew that the purpose of the nail was to place your sins where they could be hidden by his sacrifice and covered by his blood.

Jesus' forgiveness is a done deal, accomplished at Calvary. However, "Calvary's trio" of crosses reminds us we must personally accept that and embrace this gift in our lives.

Ever wonder why there were two crosses next to Christ? Why not six or ten? Ever wonder why Jesus was in the center? Why not on the far right or far left? Could it be that the two crosses on the hill symbolize one of God's greatest gifts? The gift of choice.

The two criminals have so much in common. Convicted by the same system. Condemned to the same death. Surrounded by the same crowd. Equally close to the same Jesus. In fact, they begin with the same sarcasm: "The two criminals also said cruel things to Jesus."

But one changed.

One of the criminals on a cross began to shout insults at Jesus: "Aren't you the Christ? Then save yourself and us." But the other criminal stopped him and said, "You should fear God! You are getting the same punishment he is. We are punished justly, getting what we deserve for what we did. But this man has done nothing wrong." Then he said, "Jesus, remember me when you come into your kingdom." Jesus said to him, *"I tell you the truth, today you will be with me in paradise."*

Much has been said about the prayer of the penitent thief, and it certainly warrants our admiration. But while we rejoice at the thief who changed, dare we forget the one who didn't? What about him, Jesus? Wouldn't a personal invitation be appropriate? Wouldn't a word of persuasion be timely?

There are times when God sends thunder to stir us. There are times when God sends blessings to lure us. But there are times when God sends nothing but silence as he honors us with the freedom to choose where we spend eternity.

Have we been given any greater privilege than that of choice? Not only does this privilege offset any injustice, the gift of free will can offset any mistakes.

Think about the thief who repented. Though we know little about him, we know this: He made some bad mistakes in life. He chose the wrong crowd, the wrong morals, the wrong behavior. But would you consider his life a waste? Is he spending eternity reaping the fruit of all the bad choices he made? No, just the opposite. He is enjoying the fruit of one good choice he made. In the end all his bad choices were redeemed by a solitary good one.

No matter how many bad choices you have made in the past, they are redeemed by one good choice—to follow Jesus. Will you make that choice now? Not only will your life be impacted for eternity but your life on earth will have purpose.

Jesus says, *"Here I am! I stand at the door and knock. If anyone hears my voice and opens the door, I will come in . . ."* (Revelation 3:20 NIV).

Why don't you start with your bad moments? Those bad habits? Leave them at the Cross. Your selfish moods and white lies? Give them to God. Your binges and bigotries? God wants them all. Every flop, every failure. He wants every single one. Why? Because he knows we can't live with them.

With all of my heart, I urge you to accept God's purpose for your life. According to the Bible, "Jesus is the only One who can save people. His name is the only power in the world that has been given to save people. We must be saved through him" (Acts 4:12 NCV).

Would you let him save you? This is the most important decision you will ever make. Why don't you give your heart to him right now? Admit your need. *"If we confess our sins to Him, He is faithful and just to forgive us and to cleanse us from every wrong"* (1 John 1:9 NLT). Agree that Jesus died to pay for your sins and that he rose from the dead and is alive today. *"If you confess with your mouth, 'Jesus is Lord,' and believe in your heart that God raised him from the dead, you will be saved"* (Romans 10:9 NIV).

When we were utterly helpless, Christ came at just the right time and died for us sinners. Now, most people would not be willing to die for an upright person, though someone might perhaps be willing to die for a person who is especially good. But God showed his great love for us by sending Christ to die for us while we were still sinners.

Romans 5:6–8 NLT

DOES GOD CARE?

Max Lucado
(excerpt from *Fearless*)

Fear corrodes our confidence in God's goodness. We begin to wonder if love lives in heaven. If God can sleep in our storms, if his eyes stay shut when our eyes grow wide, if he permits storms after we get on his boat, does he care? Fear unleashes a swarm of doubts, anger-stirring doubts.

And it turns us into control freaks. "Do something about the storm!" is the implicit demand of the question. "Fix it or . . . or . . . or else!" Fear, at its center, is a perceived loss of control. When life spins wildly, we grab for a component of life we can manage: our diet, the tidiness of a house, the armrest of a plane, or, in many cases, people. The more insecure we feel, the meaner we become. We growl and bare our fangs. Why? Because we are bad? In part. But also because we feel cornered.

Martin Niemöller documents an extreme example of this. He was a German pastor who took a heroic stand against Adolf Hitler. When he first met the dictator in 1933, Niemöller stood at the back of the room and listened. Later, when his wife asked him what he'd learned, he said, "I discovered that Herr Hitler is a terribly frightened man." Fear releases the tyrant within.

It also deadens our recall. The disciples had reason to trust Jesus. By now they'd seen him "healing all kinds of sickness and all kinds of disease among the people" (Matt. 4:23 NKJV). They had witnessed him heal a leper with a touch and a servant with a command (Matt. 8:3, 13 NKJV). Peter saw his sick mother-in-law recover (Matt. 8:14–15 NKJV), and they all saw demons scatter like bats out of a cave. "He cast out the spirits with a word, and healed all who were sick" (Matt. 8:16 NKJV).

Shouldn't someone mention Jesus' track record or review his résumé? Do they remember the accomplishments of Christ? They may not. Fear creates a form of spiritual amnesia. It dulls our miracle memory. It makes us forget what Jesus has done and how good God is.

And fear feels dreadful. It sucks the life out of the soul, curls us into an embryonic state, and drains us dry of contentment. We become abandoned barns, rickety and tilting from the winds, a place where humanity used to eat, thrive, and find warmth. NO longer. When fear shapes our lives, safety becomes our god. When safety becomes our god, we worship the risk-free life. Can the safety lover do anything great? Can the risk-averse accomplish noble deeds? For God? For others? No. The fear-filled cannot love deeply. Love is risky. They cannot give to the poor. Benevolence has no guarantee of return. The fear-filled cannot dream wildly. What if their dreams sputter and fall from the sky? The worship of safety emasculates greatness. No wonder Jesus wages such a war against fear.

His most common command emerges from the "fear not" genre. The Gospels list some 125 Christ-issued imperatives. Of these, 21 urge us to "not be afraid" or "not fear" or "have courage" or "take heart" or "be of good cheer." The second most common command, to love God and neighbor, appears on only eight occasions. If quantity is any indicator, Jesus takes our fears seriously. The one statement he made more than any other was this: don't be afraid . . .

So don't be afraid.

* You are worth much more than many sparrows. (Matt. 10:31 NCV) . . .
* I tell you not to worry about everyday life—whether you have enough. (Matt. 6:25 NLT) . . .
* Take courage. I am here! (Matt. 14:27 NLT)
* Do not fear those who kill the body, but cannot kill the soul. (Matt. 10:28 NKJV)
* Don't let your hearts be troubled. Trust in God, and trust also in me . . . (John 14:1 NLT)
* I will come and get you, so that you will always be with me where I am. (John 14:1, 3 NLT)
* Don't be troubled or afraid. (John 14:27 NLT) . . .
* You will hear of wars and rumors of wars, but see to it that you are not alarmed. (Matt. 24:6 NIV)
* Jesus came and touched them and said,
* "Arise, and do not be afraid." (Matt. 17:7 NKJV)

THE ULTIMATE FEAR

Max Lucado
(excerpt from *Fearless*)

Don't let your hearts be troubled.
Trust in God, and trust also in me.
(John 14:1 NLT)

Aristotle called death the thing to be feared most because "it appears to be the end of everything."[1] Jean-Paul Sartre asserted that death "removes all meaning from life."[2] Robert Green Ingersoll, one of America's most outspoken agnostics, could offer no words of hope at his brother's funeral. He said, "Life is a narrow vale between the cold and barren peaks of two eternities. We strive in vain to look beyond the heights."[3]

The pessimism of French philosopher Francois Rabelais was equally arctic. He made this sentence his final one: "I am going to the great Perhaps."

Such sad, depressing language! If death is

nothing more than "the end of everything," "barren peaks," and "the great Perhaps," what is the possibility of dying bravely? But what if the philosophers missed it? Suppose death is different than they thought, less a curse and more a passageway, not a crisis to be avoided but a corner to be turned?

This is the promise of Christ: "Don't let your hearts be troubled. Trust in God, and trust also in me. There is more than enough room in my Father's home. If this were not so, would I have told you that I am going to prepare a place for you? When everything is ready, I will come and get you, so that you will always be with me where I am" (John 14:1–3 NLT).

Have you claimed his promise?

If not, maybe it's because it sounds too good to be true.

"For God so loved the world that he gave his one and only Son, that whoever believes in him shall not perish but have eternal life" (John 3:16 NIV).

Millions read the verse. Only a handful trust it. Wary of a catch perhaps? Not needy enough maybe? Cautioned by guarded friends?

But desperation heightens interest.

Life seems to bring us to a place of desperation. Whether we are confronted with horrific acts of violence and terrorism like September 11, 2001, or catastrophic events of hurricanes, earthquakes, floods , or it may be desperation of when he asks for a divorce or she says, "It's over." When the coroner calls, the kids rebel, or the finances collapse. When desperation typhoons into your world, God's offer in John 3:16 morphs from a nice verse to a life vest.

Some of you are wearing it. You can recount the day you put it on. For you, the passage comforts like your favorite blanket:

God so loved . . .
believes in him . . .
shall not perish . . .
eternal life.

These words have kept you company though multiple windswept winters. I pray they warm you through the ones that remain. Others of you are still studying the flyer. Still pondering the possibility, wrestling with the promise. One day wondering what kind of fool offer this is, the next wondering what kind of fool would turn it down.

I urge you not to. Don't walk away from this one. Who else can get you home? Who else has turned his grave into a changing closet and offered to do the same with yours? Take Jesus' offer and you'll come to the realization that God does care, He cares so much for you that He made a way for you to live with Him forever and enjoy abundantly all that He has in store for you.

Jesus says, "I have come that they may have life, and that they may have it more abundantly" (John 10:10 NKJV).

Therefore humble yourselves under the mighty hand of God, that He may exalt you in due time, casting all your care upon Him, for He cares for you.

1 Peter 5:6–7 NKJV

And if God cares so wonderfully for wildflowers that are here today and thrown into the fire tomorrow, he will certainly care for you. Why do you have so little faith?

Matthew 6:30 NLT

Give all your worries and cares to God, for he cares about you.

1 Peter 5:7 NLT

CONFIDENT HOPE

Max Lucado
(excerpt from *Traveling Light*)

For many people, life is—well, life is a jungle. Not a jungle of trees and beasts. Would that it were so simple. Would that our jungles could be cut with a machete or our adversaries trapped in a cage. But our jungles are comprised of the thicker thickets of failing health, broken hearts, and empty wallets. Our forests are framed with hospital walls and divorce courts. We don't hear the screeching of birds or the roaring of lions, but we do hear the complaints of neighbors and the demands of bosses. Our predators are our creditors, and the brush that surrounds us is the rush that exhausts us.

It's a jungle out there.

And for some, even many, hope is in short supply . . .

What would it take to restore your hope? . . .

Our Shepherd majors in restoring hope to the soul. Whether you are a lamb lost on a craggy ledge or a city slicker alone in a deep jungle, everything changes when your rescuer appears.

Your loneliness diminishes, because you have fellowship.

Your despair decreases, because you have vision.

Your confusion begins to lift, because you have direction.

Please note: You have left the jungle. The trees still eclipse the sky, and the thorns still cut the skin. Animals lurk and rodents scurry. The jungle is still a jungle. It hasn't changed, but you have. You have changed because you have hope. And you have hope because you have met someone who can lead you out.

Your Shepherd knows that you were not made for this place. He knows you are not equipped for this place. So he has come to guide you out. He has come to restore your soul . . .

Jesus doesn't give hope by changing the jungle; he restores our hope by giving us himself. And he has promised to stay until the very end: "I am with you always, to the very end of the age" (Matt. 28:20 NIV) . . .

So Jesus' words, "I am with you always" not when you're good, not just when you pray, not when life is easy and everything seems to be going your way, but ALWAYS! It's that "ALWAYS" that gives us the confident hope that no matter what may come our way we can TRUST HIM!

Charles Stanley
(excerpt from *When Tragedy Strikes*)

We can never know what transpired in the hearts and minds of those men and women who died in the collapse of the World Trade Center buildings, but I am sure that many, knowing they were about to die, courageously committed themselves into the arms of a loving God. One whose arms were there to shield them from the steel and rubble and usher them gently to their heavenly reward.

There is an old gospel song by Charles Tindley that states, "We'll understand it better by and by." Only in eternity will we understand some of the mysterious ways of almighty God. Only then will we grasp the significance of his eternal plan that encompasses all of us.

Many of God's saints have known times of trouble and difficulty as they journeyed through life. Consider David the psalmist of Israel. Though he was anointed and chosen to be king, he found himself hated and hunted by those who sought to destroy him. In Psalm 27, however, notice what he says while in the midst of trouble:

> *The Lord is [the] light [of] my salvation;*
> *whom shall I fear?*
> *The Lord is the defense of my life;*
> *whom shall I dread?*
> *When evildoers came upon me*
> *to devour my flesh,*
> *My adversaries and my enemies,*
> *they stumbled and fell.*
> *Though a host encamp against me,*
> *my heart will not fear;*
> *though war rise against me;*
> *in spite of this I shall be confident.*
> (vv. 1–3, NASB, emphasis added)

These are the words of a man who has learned how to be sustained in the most difficult, trying times of life. He learned an amazing lesson—in the midst of tragedy, he did not need to live in fear, because God was his defense. Though in a war zone, he could be fully confident that God would protect and sustain him . . .

There is hope for us because God has promised never to leave us or to forsake us. There is hope because we are not alone— we have each other. This is the strength of a nation under attack—a united spirit gaining confidence and determination from each other. But more importantly, learning to rely on our God . . .

We are not a fearful people. We do not suddenly give up just because something frightens us. When I was about nine years old, Pearl Harbor was attacked. The American response was unforgettable. Young men, barely sixteen or seventeen years old, lined up to enlist and to serve. They did not care which branch of service would take them; they only wanted to defend their nation.

When united, this country trembles before no other power. We have a national sense of courage and bravery. We have a heritage of firmness and determination that has carried us through many troubling and dangerous times. I want to remind you of this so that none of us will expect anything less from our nation than a determined, courageous response to the task ahead. Doris Dougherty captured this moment accurately when she said, "No greater tragedy can be found than that of a soul crying out 'It's not fair!' and allowing the cold waters of cynicism to overflow and to drown him." She continues that there is no greater victory than to plunge into these waters where the bottom cannot be felt, but the strong person will "swim until I can!" We may not be able to feel the bottom right now, but our country will swim until we do!

In the 1940s America began fighting a war in the Pacific and soon thereafter a war in Europe as well. Back then, America was not heavily industrialized; we were mostly a nation of farmers. We were unprepared for war, and yet we successfully fought on two fronts for four long years. The cost was devastatingly high, but we were triumphant, which says something about our bravery, determination, and national character . . .

We have a right to be a godly people who are fearless. We have a right to be bold and confident for the simple reason that God has promised to intervene on our behalf. Does that mean that we will never suffer consequences? No, it does not. Will we always be free from hardship and adversity? Of course not. It means that when we, as individuals or as a nation, stand sovereign under the protection of God, then we can be assured that He will not fail us. No matter neither the disaster that we face nor the enemy at our gate, with God we will be triumphant.

Rejoice in our confident hope.
Be patient in trouble, and keep on praying.

Romans 12:12 NLT

I pray that your hearts will be flooded with light so that you can understand the confident hope he has given to those he called—his holy people who are his rich and glorious inheritance.

Ephesians 1:18 NLT

I pray that God, the source of hope, will fill you completely with joy and peace because you trust in him. Then you will overflow with confident hope through the power of the Holy Spirit.

Romans 15:13 NLT

LOOKING FORWARD

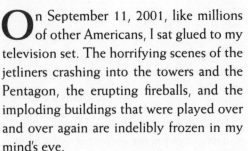

Anne Graham Lotz
(excerpt from *Heaven: My
Father's House*)

On September 11, 2001, like millions of other Americans, I sat glued to my television set. The horrifying scenes of the jetliners crashing into the towers and the Pentagon, the erupting fireballs, and the imploding buildings that were played over and over again are indelibly frozen in my mind's eye.

I wonder how many parents were faced with teary, terrified children who returned home from school that Tuesday afternoon asking, "Mommy, Daddy, are we at war? Are we going to die? Will we be safe?" How did parents answer? Did they speak the truth? Or did they just give hollow words of comfort because they had no answers?

While we cannot guarantee the safety of our children, or ourselves, or anyone else in this life, Jesus Christ does guarantee our safety in eternity. When you and I place our faith in Him as Savior and yield our lives to Him as Lord, God promises that we "shall not perish but have eternal life" (John 3:16 NIV). And the "eternal life" will be lived with God and His family in *My Father's House!* . . .

Heaven is a very real place that will give you real freedom. You need never fear . . .

hijackers or bombers, terrorists or threats, lawsuits or gunshots, bullets or bandits, boundaries that stifle, roadblocks that stop, limits that squelch, walls that strangle, planes that crash, buildings that implode . . .

The Creator Who created all the earthly beauty we have grown to love . . .

The majestic snowcapped peaks of
    the Alps,
The rushing mountain streams,
The brilliantly colored fall leaves,
The carpets of wildflowers,
The glistening fin of a fish as it leaps
    out of a sparkling sea,
The graceful gliding of a swan across
    the lake,

The lilting notes of canary's song,
The whir of a humming bird's wings,
The shimmer of the dew on the grass
in early morning . . .

If God could make the heavens and earth as beautiful as we think they are today—which includes thousands of years of wear and tear, corruption and pollution, sin and selfishness—can you imagine what the new Heaven and the new earth will look like? It will be much more glorious than any eyes have seen, any ears have heard, or any minds have ever conceived!

Death is the great equalizer, isn't it? It doesn't matter if we have lives on this earth as:

young or old
rich or poor
famous or unknown
educated or ignorant
powerful or weak
religious or atheistic
athletic or crippled
healthy or sickly
happy or depressed
we all die.

Still, death can come as an utterly unexpected surprise. More than three thousand men and women went to work at the World Trade Center in New York City on September 11, 2001, and began what they thought was just another routine day at the office. Many of them had likely gotten a cup of coffee, sat down at their desks, rolled up their sleeves, booted up their computers, and began placing telephone calls. None of them had any indication that within the hour they would step into eternity. For them, death came as a thief in the night.

For others, death can come as a longed-for and welcomed relief. Within a three-week period, while I was in the midst of writing this book, I attended both the funeral of my husband's beloved brother, John Lotz, and the funeral of my father's associate T. W. Wilson, who was like a second father to me. John died as a result of a fast-growing, malignant brain tumor. "Uncle T" died from massive heart failure at the grand old age of eight-two. For both John and uncle T, death came as an angel of mercy.

Regardless of how or when it comes, death does come for each of us. And each of us wonders: *When will it come for my loved one? What will it be like for me?*

For the past thirteen years I have traveled all over the world in response to invitations to give out God's Word. There have been times, such as my first visit to India, when I have started out by climbing onto the plane with my stomach churning, my knees knocking, and my heart fibrillating—terrified because I was not sure where I was going or who would meet me at the journey's end. But what a difference there has been in my attitude when I have had the opportunity for a second visit to that same place. I have left home with peace in my heart because I knew where I was going and who would meet me at the journey's end. In the same way, the prospect of death can fill you and me with terror and dread—unless we know where we are going. Knowing as much as we can about our final destination, and Who will meet us at the end of life's journey, takes the fear out of getting there . . .

Are you facing the future with eyes wide shut, teeth clenched, body tensed, dreading your tomorrows and what they may hold? Do you feel as though you are standing on the brink of a deep, dark abyss of helplessness and despair, caught up in events involving yourself or your loves ones that are beyond your control? Regardless of what those events may be, no matter your mental or emotional or spiritual state, God's vision of the future can fill you with hope right now . . .

As I contemplate the deaths of my loved ones—and yours . . .

As I contemplate our loss and the empty void in our hearts left by their absence . . .

I am more grateful than ever that this life is not all there is!

Praise God! You and I can look *forward WITH HOPE!* because we have the blessed assurance of Heaven, My Father's House!

"Let not your heart be troubled; you believe in God, believe also in Me. In My Father's house are many mansions; if it were not so, I would have told you. I go to prepare a place for you. And if I go and prepare a place for you, I will come again and receive you to Myself; that where I am, there you may be also. And where I go you know, and the way you know." Thomas said to Him, "Lord, we do not know where You are going, and how can we know the way?" Jesus said to him, "I am the way, the truth, and the life. No one comes to the Father except through Me.

John 14:1–7 NKJV

Never Forget ... Hope

Henri Nouwen
(excerpt from *Turn My Mourning into Dancing*)

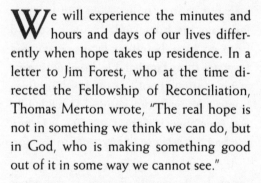

We will experience the minutes and hours and days of our lives differently when hope takes up residence. In a letter to Jim Forest, who at the time directed the Fellowship of Reconciliation, Thomas Merton wrote, "The real hope is not in something we think we can do, but in God, who is making something good out of it in some way we cannot see."

Hope is not dependent on peace in the land, justice in the world, and success in the business. Hope is willing to leave unanswered questions unanswered and unknown futures unknown. Hope makes you see God's guiding hand not only in the gentle and pleasant moments but also in the shadows of disappointment and darkness.

No one can truly say with certainty where he or she will be ten or twenty years from now. You do not know if you will be free or in captivity, if you will be honored or despised, if you have many friends or few, if you will be liked or rejected. But when you hold lightly these dreams and fears, you can be open to receive every day as a new day and to live your life as a unique expression of God's love for humankind . . .

A soldier was captured as a prisoner of war. His captors transported him by train far from his homeland. He felt isolated from country, bereft of family, estranged from anything familiar. His loneliness grew as he continued not to hear anything from home. He could not know that his family was even alive, how his country was faring. He had lost a sense of anything to live for.

But suddenly, unexpectedly, he got a letter. It was smudged, torn at the edges from months of travel. But it said, "We are waiting for you to come home. All is fine here. Don't worry." Everything instantly seemed different. His circumstances had not changed. He did the same difficult labor on the same merger rations, but now he knew someone waited for his release and homecoming. Hope changed his life.

God has written us a letter. The good news of God's revelation in Christ declares to us precisely what we need to hope. Sometimes the words of the Bible do not seem important to us. Or they do not appeal to us. But in those words we hear Christ saying in effect, "I am preparing a house for you and there are many rooms in my house." Paul the Apostle tells us, "Be transformed by the renewing of your minds" (Romans 12:2 NRSV). We hear a promise and an invitation to a life we could not dream of if all we considered were our own resources.

Therein is the hope that gives us new power to live, new strength. We find a way, even in sadness and illness and even death, never to forget how we can hope.

We catch glimmers of this way to live even while we must admit how dimly we see it and imperfectly we live it. "I am holding on to my conviction that I can trust God," I must tell myself sometimes, "since I cannot . . . yet say it fully." I dare to say it even when everything is not perfect, when I know others will criticize my actions, when I fear that my limitations will disappoint many—and myself. But still I trust that the truth will shine through, even when I cannot fully grasp it. Still I believe that God will accomplish what I cannot, in God's own grace and unfathomable might.

The paradox of expectation is that those who believe in tomorrow can better live today; those who expect joy to come out of sadness can discover the beginnings of a new life amid the old; those who look forward to the returning Lord can discover him already in their midst. Just as the love of a mother for her son can grow while she is waiting for his return, just as lovers can rediscover each other after long periods of absence, so our intimate relationship with God can become deeper and more mature while we wait patiently in expectation of his return.

To hope for this growth, to believe even in its possibility, is to say no to every form of fatalism. Is to voice a no to every way we tell ourselves "I know myself—I cannot expect any changes." This no to discouragement and self-despair comes in the context of a yes to life, a yes we say amid even fragile times lived in a world of impatience and violence. For even while we mourn, we do not forget how our life can ultimately join God's larger dance of life and hope.

God is our refuge and strength, a very present
    help in trouble.
Therefore we will not fear, even though the earth
    be removed,
And though the mountains be carried into the
    midst of the sea;
Though its waters roar and be troubled, though
    the mountains shake with it swelling.
There is a river whose streams shall make
    glad the city of God,

the holy place of the tabernacle of the Most High.
God is in the midst of her, she shall not be moved;
God shall help her, just at the break of dawn.
The nations raged, the kingdoms were moved;
He uttered His voice, the earth melted.
The Lord of hosts is with us; the God of Jacob
    is our refuge. (Selah)
Come, behold the works of the Lord, who has made
desolations in the earth. He makes wars
    cease to the
end of the earth; He breaks the bow and cuts
    the spear
in two; He burns the chariot in the fire.
Be still, and know that I am God; I will be
    exalted among the nations,
I will be exalted in the earth!
The Lord of hosts is with us; the God of
    Jacob is our refuge.

Psalm 46 NKJV

I pray that God, the source of hope,
will fill you completely with joy and peace
because you trust in him.
Then you will overflow with confident hope
through the power of the Holy Spirit.

Romans 15:13 NLT

NOTES

[1]Donald G. Bloesch, *The Last Things: Resurrection, Judgment, Glory* (Downers Grove, IL: InterVarsity Press, 2004), 125

[2]Ibid.

[3]John Blanchard, *Whatever Happened to Hell?* (Wheaton, IL: Crossway Books, 1995), 63.

Prayers for
. . . HOPE

_____

_____

_____

_____

_____

_____

_____

_____

_____

_____

_____

_____

_____

_____

_____

_____

✶ ✶ ✶ ✶ ✶

Prayers for
... HOPE

_____

_____

_____

_____

_____

_____

_____

_____

_____

_____

_____

_____

_____

_____

_____

★ ★ ★ ★ ★

Prayers for
. . . HOPE

_____

_____

_____

_____

_____

_____

_____

_____

_____

_____

_____

_____

_____

_____

_____

_____

★ ★ ★ ★ ★

Prayers for
. . . HOPE

_____

_____

_____

_____

_____

_____

_____

_____

_____

_____

_____

_____

_____

_____

_____

_____

_____

★ ★ ★ ★ ★

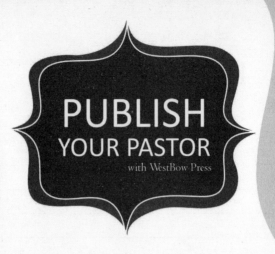